D0819631

Published 1999 by Grolier Educational
Sherman Turnpike, Danbury, Connecticut.
Copyright © 1999 Times Editions Pte Ltd. Singapore.

Set ISBN: 0-7172-9324-6
Volume ISBN: 0-7172-9325-4

CIP information available from the Library of Congress or the publisher

Brown Partworks Ltd.

Series Editor: Tessa Paul
Series Designer: Joyce Mason
Crafts devised and created by Susan Moxley
Music arrangements by Harry Boteler
Photographs by Bruce Mackie
Production: Alex Mackenzie
Stylists: Joyce Mason and Tessa Paul

For this volume:
Writer: Hannah Beardon
Consultant: Héctor Férnandes
Editorial Assistants: Hannah Beardon and Paul Thompson

Printed in Italy

Adult supervision advised for all crafts and recipes, particularly those involving sharp instruments and heat.

CONTENTS

BOLIVIA:

Bolivia is a landlocked country. This means that it is surrounded by other countries and has no coastline. It lies within the tropical region of South America.

▼ **The geography** of Bolivia ranges from high mountain ranges to the low-lying jungles of the Amazon River. The landscape is sometimes harsh, but it is also majestic.

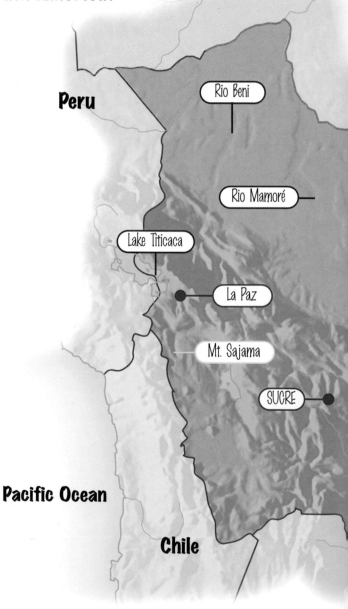

Peru

Rio Beni

Rio Mamoré

Lake Titicaca

La Paz

Mt. Sajama

SUCRE

Pacific Ocean

Chile

◄ **The churches** of Bolivia were built mostly by the Catholic Church during colonial times. The decoration often combines Christian images with those of earlier, local gods. The domes and bell towers of these churches stand high above the low buildings found in most Bolivian towns and cities.

Brazil

Bolivia

Santa Cruz

Paraguay

Argentina

First Impressions

- **Population** 6,440,000
- **Largest city** La Paz with a population of 1,013,688
- **Longest river** Rio Mamoré, which flows into the Amazon
- **Highest mountain** Mt Sajama at 21,463 ft.
- **Exports** Natural gas, tin, silver, zinc, and coffee
- **Capital city** Sucre is the legal capital, but La Paz is the main center
- **Political status** Republic
- **Climate** Wide range, from hot and humid to arctic cold
- **Art and culture** Bolivia is well known for its haunting traditional folk music and its colorful woven textiles with geometric patterns.

◄ **Lake Titicaca** lies on the border between Peru and Bolivia. It is 12,500 feet above sea level. It is so deep that for a long time it was described as "bottomless." Now we know that it is over 900 feet deep. For hundreds of years the local people have woven their boats from reeds. Fishermen on this lake still construct these unusual craft.

RELIGIONS

Most Bolivians are Roman Catholics, but their beliefs are often mixed with the ancient native religions of the Incas.

THE PEOPLE WHO lived in Bolivia before the Spanish arrived belonged to many different religious and cultural groups. The most powerful were the Quechua-speaking Incas who ruled the country, but the Aymaras and the Guaranis also lived there.

When the Spanish arrived 500 years ago, they tried to abolish the religion of the Incas and make everyone become Catholic. But the Incas worshipped many gods and were able to include the Christian god among them. When the Spanish saw that the Incas were worshipping the Christian god, they began to believe that the old religion had disappeared, but many elements of it remain to this day.

Religion in Bolivia is part of everyday life. Most of the festivals you will read about are religious. The majority of these are on Catholic feast days, while others date back to before the Spanish arrived. There seems to be a festival just about every day of the year.

GREETINGS FROM **BOLIVIA!**

In modern Bolivia Spanish is the official language. Most people speak it. However, over a third of the people still speak Quechua, the ancient language of the Incas, and nearly a quarter speak Aymara, another ancient Indian language. Until the Spanish arrived, Indian languages were not written down. Much of their history was recorded verbally in myths and legends. Often these languages were recorded and given a written vocabulary by the priests who brought Christianity to Bolivia. The expressions given here are in Spanish.

How do you say...

Hello

¡Hola!

How are you?

¿Como está usted?

My name is

Me llamo

Goodbye

Adios

Thank you

Gracias

Peace

La paz

ALASITAS

On January 24 every year the people of La Paz have a big market called Alasitas. People buy tiny models and statues for Ekeko, the Aymara god of abundance.

The word *Ekeko* means "dwarf" in the Aymaran language. Almost every house in La Paz has a statue of Ekeko carrying sacks of rice, sugar, and flour and miniatures of household objects. On January 24 people buy miniature models of things that they wish they had. They give these models to the little god. They believe that Ekeko will one day help them to own the real version. A lot of people buy cases of tiny dollar bills, too, hoping that they will get rich.

When the Spanish took control, they banned all the native religious rituals including those for

If someone wants a house, they buy a little model of a house and give it to Ekeko. People believe that if they honor Ekeko, they will never fall on hard times and their home will always be happy.

Ekeko they call you in Alasitas of La Paz. Everybody wants you to themselves because you are happiness. Children come to laugh, and grownups come to listen and admire your smallness because in the world there is no other like you, nor will there be in your old age another power so great.

Ekeko. In 1781 the Spanish ruler of La Paz started a festival to honor the Virgin of La Paz. The people began to identify this new festival with the old celebrations for Ekeko.

Now each year on Alasitas Day a market sets up in La Paz that sells miniature versions of things. Fake banks supplying fake Alasitas money appear in the market. These little goods and bank notes are sold to be placed on or around the statues of Ekeko.

EKEKO

E - ke - ko te lla - han a ti en a - la - ci - tas
To dos - te bus - can pa ra si por - que eres la fe -

de La Paz. Y ni - nos vie - nen a re - ir
li - ci - dad.

y vie - jos vie - nen a es - cu - char ad mi rar tu pe que nes

por - que en el mun - do No hay o - troi - gual ni ve - ran

en tu ve - jez o - tro po - der tan co co cal.

CANDELARIA

Candelaria *means Candlemas Day. This is on February 2, and it is a celebration of the purification of the Virgin Mary. Processions and prayers mark this special occasion.*

Candlemas Day is a Christian festival that takes place 40 days after Christmas. This marks the time that Mary took the Baby Jesus to the Jewish Temple where both mother and son were blessed.

In Bolivia there are many statues of the purified Virgin and her child, but the one in the city of Copacabana is believed to be very powerful. People say she performs miracles, helping people solve their problems when no one else can.

On Candlemas Day the statue of the Copacabana Virgin is beautifully dressed in precious robes and jewels. Crowds line the streets to see her on this day.

Below is a shrine for the Virgin of Candlemas. In front of her image people place models of things that they would like to have in the coming year.

STUFFED AVOCADOS

SERVES 6

3 avocados
2 tomatoes, chopped
1 small onion, chopped
1/2 green pepper, diced
1 t. lemon juice
1 t. oil
salt and pepper

Cut the avocados in half and remove the stones. Stir the tomatoes, onion, capsicums, lemon juice, and oil together in a small bowl. Season with salt and pepper to taste. Mix well. Spoon about one sixth of the tomato mixture into the center of each avocado half. Serve immediately.

Pilgrims walk many miles from all over Bolivia to prove their devotion to the Virgin. Pilgrims are people who visit holy places. Many pilgrims carry heavy objects to make the journey difficult. They show their faith and gratitude through this physical suffering.

At midday priests dressed in silver and gold lead a procession from the church through the main streets of the town. The priests are accompanied by dance troupes and pilgrims. The statue always stays in the church, so the priests carry a replica surrounded by flowers and candles.

People try to touch the statue and ask it for its blessing. They also ask Mary for help with their problems.

The processional route is decorated with multicolored cloth, flowers, and anything made of silver, such as cutlery.

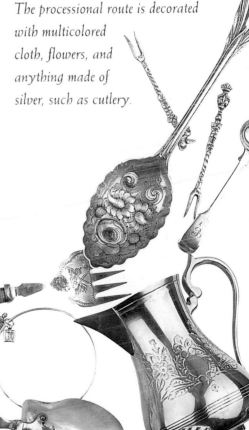

THE VIRGIN OF THE CAVE

Bolivians commemorate the kindness and generosity of the Virgin during the carnival of Oruro.

ONCE UPON A TIME a wicked bandit called Chiru-Chiru lived in a cave near the town of Oruro. When he was hungry, he didn't bother to go to work like everybody else. Instead he would creep out into the night to attack passing travelers and salesmen and steal their money. Then he would go into Oruro, and with his loot he would buy his food and something to drink.

Chiru-Chiru lived well like this for years, and he always gave thanks to the Blessed Virgin Mary for his good luck.

Then one night the outlaw met his match. He was sitting in his cave when he heard the sound of horses' hooves. Chiru-Chiru slipped out and hid in some trees. From behind the trees he saw a carriage coming around the corner. Quickly he stepped out into the road.

"Stand and deliver!" he cried. But for once Chiru-Chiru had made a mistake. His victim was quick-witted and strong. He stabbed Chiru-Chiru, who fell to the ground, dying.

The woods that Chiru-Chiru knew so well seemed dark and scary, and he called to his beloved Virgin for help. She heard his pleas, and even though he was a bad man, she came to him. She led him

back to his cave and comforted him as he lay dying. With his last breath the bandit thanked and blessed the Virgin Mary.

Days went by, and gradually the people of Oruro realized that Chiru-Chiru was missing. Most people were too scared to go near his cave, but the bravest people from the town offered to go and see what the bandit was doing. When they reached the cave, they found Chiru-Chiru dead. They were amazed by a vision that hovered above his head. They saw a shining image of the Virgin Mary, and she was carrying the Baby Jesus in her arms. From miles around folk came to see this miracle. The people of the town decided to build a church in memory of the bandit Chiru-Chiru, who died in the miraculous presence of the Virgin of the Cave.

CARNIVAL

People all over Bolivia celebrate the last days before Lent with big street parties. The most extravagant and colorful carnival is in Oruro. It is known as the Devil's Carnival.

The multicolored carnival masks cannot be taken off until the dancers reach the church.

Carnival mood takes over the Roman Catholic Christian world in the days leading up to Lent. This season of Lent lasts 40 days, and during this time Christians are expected to fast. This means they have to give up some of their favorite foods. Carnival is an opportunity to have some fun before the long period of fasting.

In Oruro the main procession lasts for 12 hours. It is led by local political and religious dignitaries carrying a statue of the Virgin of

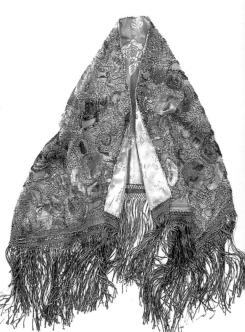

The carnival dancers wear richly embroidered costumes.

CHICKEN PIE WITH CORN TOPPING

SERVES 6 TO 8
1 onion, chopped
3 T. oil
2 lb. chicken, cubed
4 T. raisins
1 can chopped tomatoes
¼ t. cinnamon
2 hard-boiled eggs, chopped

TOPPING
1 can creamed corn
2 T. melted butter
2 eggs, beaten
paprika

Sauté the onion in the oil until soft, then add the chicken and cook for 5 minutes. Add the raisins, tomatoes, and cinnamon. Simmer for 20 minutes. Stir in the eggs and pour into a greased 3-pint soufflé dish. To make the topping, heat the corn and butter until bubbling hot. Turn the heat down and add the eggs gradually, stirring constantly. When the mixture is thick, pour over the chicken. Sprinkle with paprika and bake at 350°F for 1 hour. Serve hot.

the Cave. The theme of the procession is the battle between good and evil. Performers enact a dance in which the archangel Saint Michael wages war with devils, condors, and bears. In the Bible Saint Michael wins a fight against the devil.

Other dances show events taken from history. "*La Morenda*" and "*La Saya*" are dances that tell the story of the Africans brought to Bolivia by the Spanish during the seventeenth century to work as slaves in the mines of South America.

Finally, a Mass is held for the Virgin. Hymns are sung and prayers said in Quechua and in Spanish.

Carnival ends on Sunday when there is a pageant for the children and a beauty contest. Finally carnival is over – until the next year of course!

A bright embroidered cloth shows the great Andes mountains that run through Bolivia.

PHUJLLAY

Phujllay *is a Quechua word meaning "play." For two days every March thousands of peasants dressed in traditional costumes pour into the village of Tarabuco for one of Bolivia's biggest festivals.*

In 1816 the people of Bolivia were fighting against their Spanish rulers for independence. In the village of Tarabuco there was a woman named Juana Azurduy de Padilla. She led her people successfully against the Spanish. They won the Battle of Jumbati, and so liberated their village.

Nowadays country people travel many miles from the villages surrounding Tarabuco to attend this festival and give thanks for their freedom. As they go, they play traditional instruments and sing and dance to the tunes.

The festival-goers wear costumes that look like cartoon copies of the clothes worn by the Spanish invaders. Sequinned hats with feathers are made to look like Spanish war helmets.

The first day of the festival begins with a

Many traditional instruments are played during Phujllay. The Zamponas are panpipes made of bamboo.

Mass held in the open air. It is given in the Quechua language. Afterward everyone forms a procession and carries an image of Christ through the streets of the village.

After the procession there is a ceremony called *Pukhara,* which means "thanksgiving." This time people pay tribute to everyone who lost their lives in the Battle of Jumbati and give thanks to the earth for providing them with the food they eat.

Every Phujllay has a sponsor, who is called the *Alferez.* The festival-goers choose the new Alferez on the last day of Phujllay. One of the duties of the Alferez is to collect crops to be used as offerings and to have them blessed.

People buy traditional ponchos and weavings at local markets during Phujllay. They also buy musical instruments and food and drink.

MAKE A CLAY TRUCK

Clay is often used in Bolivia to make models of things that people would like to have in real life. You can make a clay model truck and fill it with food and chickens.

Trucks are an important form of transport in rural Bolivia. For many small towns and villages they act as traveling stores that supply food, clothes, and even the mail. People use them as buses to travel from town to town. During festivals they are packed full of people traveling to the celebrations, or of goods to sell at the festival.

YOU WILL NEED

Air-hardening clay
White emulsion paint
Poster paint
All-purpose glue
Water

1 Make the base of the truck. This should be about 5" long. Add the back of the truck and mold a driver. Put the driver in place. Make the wheels and cut four spaces in the sides of the truck where the wheels will be attached.

2 To attach the wheels, scratch surface of the truck where the wheels are going to fit and scratch the back of the wheels. Wet both surfaces with a little water and press together.

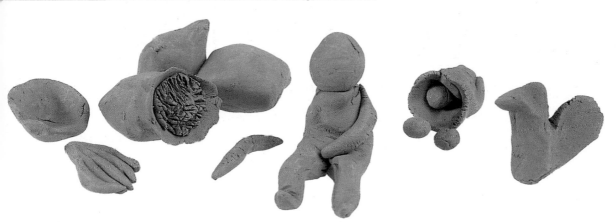

3 Add the roof of the truck. Allow the truck to dry and then paint it with white emulsion paints. When this has dried, paint the truck with poster paints. Make things to put in the truck, such as vegetables, fruit, animals, and a person. Make sure they fit. When they have dried, paint them with white emulsion paint. Allow the emulsion paint to dry and then paint them with bright poster paints.

4 Place the vegetables, fruit, and so on in the truck. Paint the whole model with all-purpose glue. This will hold the objects in place, and it will also varnish and seal the model. You now have a model of a Bolivian truck.

GRAN PODER

For ten days every June the people of La Paz celebrate **Señor del Gran Poder,** *which means "Lord of Great Power." People come from miles around to enjoy the carnival.*

The Gran Poder festival started in the 1920s. In the La Paz neighborhood of Chijini someone found a beautiful image of Jesus Christ in a house. Nobody knew where this image came from or who might have painted it. However, many local people began to believe that the image was able to perform miracles. This means they believed it cured illness.

People wear masks and ostrich-feather crowns while musicians play panpipes, guitars, and drums.

The people of Chijini named the image for its wonderful powers and lovingly placed it in their local chapel. A few years later some priests from Chijini built another, grander, chapel nearby

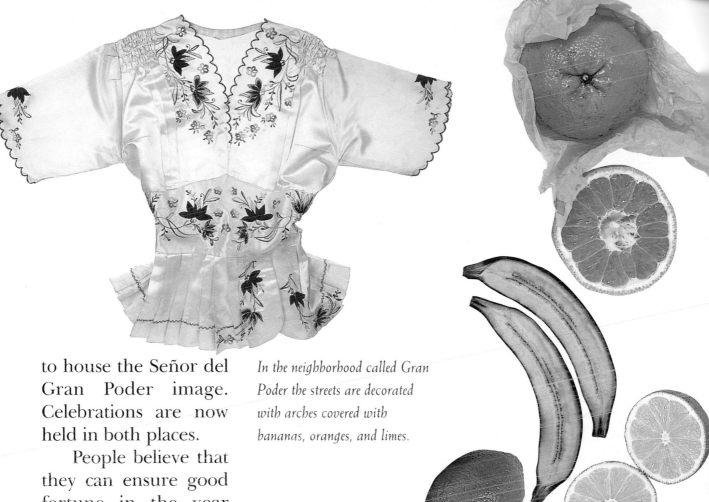

In the neighborhood called Gran Poder the streets are decorated with arches covered with bananas, oranges, and limes.

to house the Señor del Gran Poder image. Celebrations are now held in both places.

People believe that they can ensure good fortune in the year ahead by showing their deep devotion to Jesus Christ. They get up early, at 5 o'clock in the morning, to go to the first of six Masses.

After the last Mass in the old chapel priests and important locals, such as the mayor, carry the image around town on a platform of flowers and candles. Their journey ends at the new chapel.

THE THREE FACES OF CHRIST

The image of Señor del Gran Poder is unusual because it shows three faces of Jesus Christ. There is a superstition about directing prayers toward particular faces of the painting. People believe that if you want a nice thing to happen to someone else, you must pray to the face on the right of the image, but if you want to punish someone, you pray to the face on the left. If you want something for yourself, you must ask the face in the middle.

21

Urkupina

For three days every August Calvario Hill in the center of Bolivia swarms with people. They have come to this spot to commemorate a vision of the Virgin.

Many years ago a little girl from the town of Quillacollo was on a hillside where she was looking after her family's flock of llamas. Suddenly, she had a vision. On the top of Calvario Hill she could see the Virgin Mary holding the Baby Jesus. The little girl cried out loud, "Urkupina!" This word means "there on the hill." Hearing her cry, her family ran to join her. They found a big stone that looked like the Virgin. They took it to the village church and called it Urkupina.

As people heard about this miracle, they

The Virgin Mary plays an important role in Bolivian religious life. There have been many sightings of her and many people are devoted to her.

began to make trips to Calvario Hill. Now many people from all over the continent take part in this pilgrimage between August 15 and 18. They offer flowers, candles, and money to the Virgin. August 15 is also the Day of the Assumption, when all Catholics celebrate Mary's journey to heaven. Most people attend one of the hourly Masses in the local church. Colorful groups of dancers form a procession going up the hill.

People believe that any rock found on Calvario Hill has holy powers. Many people follow the custom of

striking the hillside three times with a hammer or pickax to hack off a piece of rock, which they then have blessed. They believe that the size of the rock they get decides how lucky and rich they will be in the following year.

In parts of Bolivia the high mountain air can be very cold. Women wear hats and woolen shawls to keep warm.

Bolivian people wear colorful clothing that dates back to the days before the Spanish arrived. Their clothes also show Spanish influence.

MAKE A FABRIC PICTURE

The fabrics of Bolivia are bright and colorful.
Many are woven by the people and not by factory
machines. The fabrics are used for clothes,
blankets, and to make pretty pictures.

Craftspeople do not like to waste anything. When someone has spent a long time weaving lengths of cloth, it is not easy to throw away any of that work. Scraps of fabric can be cut and stitched to make colorful patterns or images. This kind of craft is called appliqué work. Copy our fabric picture or make your own design.

YOU WILL NEED
Large square of yellow felt
Scraps of colored fabrics
Colored threads and needle
Cotton balls
Scissors
6 strands (each 5") of black yarn
Strand of red yarn
Paper and pencil

1 Plan the design on paper. Draw llama on separate sheet. Pin llama to fabric and cut around llama outline. Cut out a second llama. Cut out other fabric shapes by freehand.

2 To make hair, gather black yarn and tie together at one end with red yarn. Divide strands into three pairs, then braid together. Tie the other end with red yarn. For baby's blanket, fold an oblong of fabric into a triangle. Pin to hold shape.

3 Pin your shapes in position to form the picture. Start with the sky and move down — pin clouds, then hills, then house, and so on. Then stitch on the shapes (except the clouds and llamas) to fix them.

4 Stitch the bottom edge of the clouds, then pack in some cotton balls. Stitch the top edges. Repeat this with the llama shapes. Attach the baby's blanket with three or four stitches at top, so blanket hangs free.

5 Stitch the design onto yellow felt. Use blanket stitch (see inset). Push needle through cloth so thread forms a loop. Push needle through loop. Repeat. Decorate shapes, and make faces, with a variety of stitches.

NAVIDAD

Navidad *is the Spanish word for Christmas.*
This day is celebrated all over the Christian
world to commemorate the birth of Jesus. It
is a time for love and peace.

Christmas in Bolivia is celebrated on December 24, Christmas Eve, but the preparations begin weeks before. In the week before Christmas people put a nativity scene in their houses. This model scene shows the Baby Jesus with the Virgin Mary, Joseph, and the Three Wise Men carrying flowers and gifts, all surrounded by fruit trees. People also make clay models of things they would like to have and put them at Jesus's feet. Many people believe that at midnight, when Jesus was born, He will see the things and bless them, and their wishes will come true.

Groups of children get together and go from house to house singing adoration to Jesus. They play the harmonica and make flutes out of old tin cans and rattles out of bottle tops. In the past

Children hope presents will be left in their
shoes. Some may choose decorated
stockings to hang at the end of their
beds for Jesus to fill with presents.

people used to give the children pears, but now everyone gives them money.

Christmas Eve is a time for the family to be together. If someone doesn't have a family or a home, any household might invite them in to spend Christmas with them. At midnight everyone hugs and wishes each other happiness and peace. Then little candles are lit for Jesus. Some people go to midnight Mass to remember the birth of Christ. They call this mass "rooster Mass" because it was the rooster who told the other animals that Christ had been born, and some people even take their roosters with them to the church.

The traditional Christmas Dinner is called *Picana*, a spicy soup with plenty of chicken, corn, potatoes, and meat. Everyone is hungry because they don't eat dinner until after midnight!

After dinner the children go to bed. They leave their shoes next to the window. If they have been good, the Baby Jesus will come and fill the shoes with Christmas presents.

Everyone opens their presents in the morning. For breakfast they eat donuts and drink hot chocolate.

Christmas doesn't end until January 6. Then the family puts away the nativity scene and all the decorations until next December.

In this nativity scene a llama greets the Baby Jesus.

A CHRISTMAS TALE

This is a little story to remind children that they must be good at Christmas time.

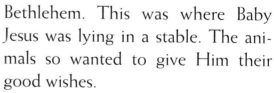

A VERY LONG time ago all the animals were equal. None was grander, or more lowly, than the other. They all lived together as friends. One dark night they were all asleep in their barnyard. It was midnight, and a brilliant star shone in the black sky. Suddenly, there was a great commotion among them.

"Cock-a-doodle-doo! Cock-a-doodle-doo!" cried the Rooster. "Christ is born!"

By now the sleepiest animals were awake. "Baa, baaa!" said the sheep. "Let's go and see!" The cows said "Moo!" They all meant "Yes, yes." So they set off following the bright star that led them to Bethlehem. This was where Baby Jesus was lying in a stable. The animals so wanted to give Him their good wishes.

It was a long journey to Bethlehem, but nobody stopped because they were longing to see the Divine Baby. Nobody, that is, except the little pigs. They were very greedy

animals. When they passed food, they forgot about the Baby and stopped to eat their fill.

The other animals were cross and shouted at the pigs to hurry and continue the journey.

"Oink, oink!" said the pigs. "Leave us to finish our dinner!" So the animals went on their way to Bethlehem without the pigs.

At last they arrived at the humble stable where Jesus lay. All the animals wanted to kiss the new Baby. All, that is, except the mule, who was bad-tempered and stubborn. When the mule saw the Baby Jesus, he caused a great big hullabaloo, bucking and kicking. He nearly knocked Jesus out of His manger. He even laughed at everyone who had come to see the Baby. "Eee-aww, eee-aww!" This was the rude sound the mule made.

To this day these disrespectful animals suffer for their bad behavior on the first Night of Christmas. Never again will the pigs be able to look up at the heavens, for if they do, they will die. And the mules will never be able to have their own children.

PATRON SAINT FESTIVAL

All the towns and villages in Bolivia have their own patron saints. Each saint has a feast day. Everyone celebrates the saint's day with fun and games, music, and dancing.

On the day of their patron saint the entire village gathers to celebrate. Those who can't go home will also have parties, even if they are living in New York or London!

The people of San Ignacio de Moxos, a town in northern Bolivia, celebrate their saint's day with a *jocheo*. This means that people are chased through the streets of the town by bulls. A favorite game during this festival is climbing the greased pole. Prizes are given to those who can reach the top.

WORDS TO KNOW

Carnival: Festivities that take place in the period before Lent in Roman Catholic countries.

Dignitary: A person who holds an important position or title, such as a politician, a bishop, or a lord.

Fast: To deliberately go without some or all kinds of food and drink .

Feast day: A day on which a religious event or the life of a saint is celebrated.

Inca: The people who ruled over a large part of South America before the arrival of the Spanish.

Independent: Self-governing, not ruled over by others.

Lent: The 40 days between Ash Wednesday and Easter.

Mass: A Christian service in which bread and wine are used to commemorate the Last Supper of Jesus Christ.

Mule: The offspring of a donkey and a horse.

Nativity: A model of the birth of Jesus.

Patron saint: A saint who is special to a particular group. Nations, towns, and professions all have patron saints.

Pilgrim: A person who makes a religious journey, or pilgrimage, to a holy place.

Poncho: A traditional Bolivian garment. A poncho is a blanketlike cloak with a hole in the middle for the head.

Roman Catholic: A member of the Roman Catholic Church, the largest branch of Christianity. The head of this church is the pope.

Saint: A title given to very holy people by some Christian churches. Saints are important in the Roman Catholic Church.

Shrine: A place that is sacred to the memory of a holy person.

Slave: A person who is, by law, owned by another person.

ACKNOWLEDGMENTS

WITH THANKS TO:
Zulema Cuenca, Vicky Céspedes, Luis Gotérrez, and Doris Gómez. Tumi, South American Crafts, London.

PHOTOGRAPHY:
All photographs by Bruce Mackie except: John Elliott pp. 11, 15. Cover photograph by Image Bank/Thomas Rampy.

ILLUSTRATIONS BY:
Fiona Saunders pp. 4 – 5. Tracy Rich p. 7.
Maps by John Woolford.

Recipes: Ellen Dupont.

SET CONTENTS